Of Violent Delights

Of Violent Delights

Dakota Minnie Boyer

More by Dakota Boyer:

Edge of Stardust

For Calliope & Circe

"These violent delights have violent ends
and in their triumph die, like fire and powder,
Which, as they kiss, consume."
-Shakespeare's *Romeo and Juliet,*
Act 2 Scene 6

Contents:

Part One: Monsters & Men

Zodiac..13

Thus Spoke Ego.....................................16

Not Like Other Girls...............................18

Supernova..20

Damsel..21

Sisters of the Swan................................23

Soul of the Sea......................................25

Stolen..26

Florida..27

Star Catcher..28

The Violinist..29

Labyrinth..31

Part Two: Interludes

Thoughts from the Boat......................34

Unrequited..35

Psyche..36

At the Sea Shore..................................38

12:16am..39

A Letter from the Sea..........................40

The Demigods..42

Empty...44

Of a Virgo..45

For a Dog...46

I Don't Write That Way....................................47

Part Three: Rage & the Valley

Off to Young Girls, Every One..........................51

Call Me as I Am..52

Sword in the Forge...54

When I Was the Tree and You Were the Sky...55

Mixed...56

Return to the Forest..58

Response to the Sound of Trees.......................59

Romeo & Juliet..60

Ally..61

No Return Receipt..63

In the Valley of the Dead.................................65

America..67

To the Conquistador..68

End of an Era..69

Glossary..71

Part One:

Monsters & Men

Zodiac

They say what a silly thing
it is to prod upon a character,
pull out strengths, pronounce desires
by how the sun kissed a child upon their
Earth side arrival, but still I ask:
How did Luna swaddle you those first nights?
Did Venus peak out from midnight cloud
to witness your flushed cheeks snuggled,
tiny fingers poking from a hospital blanket?
Who are you? I fight chaos to know
where you'll align yourself in my path.

Were you blessed by the sun's
late spring romp, rising ever higher
into the heavens each passing moment?
>[I wonder, if he was free, would he continue
>growing into infinity, ride away into the
>darkness of space like a Cancer I know?
>Or is he a good man, honest and simple?
>Does the sun care to rise each day for us below?
>Are we his duty- his charge?]

You hold fast to your greed-
living death pinned in place of a heart,
a dead weight hoisting souls over the waterfall
ready to d
        r
                o
                        p,
I fear the mangled shape of them
forever married to the bottom of the pit.
I know the hunger of your kind,

cursed in your charm, the worst being the rat.

Or are you an Autumnal tide I can't cast away,
echoing back for an occasional visit?
If so, come, let us talk until my memory catches up,
her hand on my shoulder, her breath in my ear
whispering "you don't know what's hidden."
And I don't. Never in all those momentary doses
do I find what's tucked far below- behind
a curious smile, baby doll eyes blinking fearless.
I hope for the best, anticipating your arrival again.

Maybe you're one of the tricky bunch, born first of the year.
Those few of words, but always thinking-
a massive coil of a mind spinning round and around.
They are that which take vacations upon
the sands of their mind, lost mid sentence.
I will never understand why they don't pull the coil up,
allow the weight of it to unravel itself- spill it's secrets
on the floor like Caesar's blood painting the tile.
Let it be over with one swift movement-
no "et, tu" the knife in Brutus' hand says enough
for a century of friends to look twice upon the other.
> [There is no wonder in why
> Capricorns flee from me, they ask
> what music can come of an Agate
> and I say, stones cannot sing.]

Or may you be a Leo?
So many in our number, I should learn to expect
how abundantly we sprout in August's glory
singing "praise the self, praise be me! Praise be me!"
I welcome you to flaunt your pride, stronger than Heracles
we hold up the sun for Atlas to bow down with the Earth.

We are made from stars and when we fall,
we bleed starlight so pure Polaris cries-
beautiful, we pull Narcissus from his pool.

I recognize the many other shades of life
looking out from their constellations.
I dream of those ghosts, yet they remain unfathomable
whispers floating through me, all those *others*.
I witness their star scooting past my disaster.
I hope they enjoy the show.

Thus Spoke Ego

I heard you calling on mountaintop
their curses echoing back from below.
I followed their footsteps through the meadow
flush with daisies, children making chains
adorning another, playing fairies in April rain.

Past the statues beckoning for heaven
their flags raised to the sky, torches ablaze
wishing their men back from across seas-
the Fates never wrote their footprints on those sands,
but there they end, muddled together with children
who will never know the forests where ours run
among the wolves, the roly polys and the ferns.
I blink away their cries, forced to reconcile that
I cannot enact their revenge, my anger pushed
further below, holding together in chains
like Cerberus guarding the dead
not even Orpheus can subdue.

Then there's you, high on the mountain
staring down on us below,
I confused their pleading as curses,
their words now echo through me,
as a million pure white hands wash over me,
pushing me forward so that there is only you
between me and endless sky.
I will listen.
There must be truth for you to stand
so close to the stars, your words could only drip
gold as Helios whispers them to you.
"Speak these words," he says, brilliant phrases

to praise and please, to lead us to victories
we cannot yet see....

> *"Why are we having*
> *all these people from*
> *shithole countries*
> *come here?"*

Yet, I am wrong.

> *"Get the son of a bitch*
> *off the field right now...*
> *You're fired!"*

You are only yelling,
it was your voice breaking against stone,
filtering out into the forest past.
How could their words give such a thunder?

> *"When you're a star,*
> *they let you do it."*

I breathe my thought, preparing for
my own voice only to realize you are lost.
Your birth placed you too close to the stars,
you could never feel the earth's humble
caress to dirty feet and I cannot find a reason
to subject my heart to your cackling.

Breaking away from the crowd,
their hands no longer grip to me,
"but he is the Uber mich," they say.
No, he is but a man pretending God.

Not Like Other Girls

God of the sea,
such shame an ocean of beauty
reflects no change to his temperament-
He chooses to be the storm.
Why feign ignorance, Athena?
All the naiads know what follow his sails,
and his sights were set on her for weeks.
He knew her shadow along the marble,
her laugh against the seashore.
He was determined and like June rain,
he struck without warning,
just as he came for you.

She was your own,
yet you brutalized amidst despair-
cursed her when she was not to blame.
You knew, she could not outlast the struggle-
the unrelenting beat of his waves,
and for all her years devoted,
you threw her out for the embarrassment.
                {What would they say?
                Oh, didn't you hear?
                Poseidon bested Athena.
                Silly girl. Silly girl.}

May Alethea point poised fingers to you,
whisper amongst the Muses, the Furies,
and the nymphs- let them coil horror from your deeds:
how a monster stalks alone for your ego,
no reflection capable of holding her gaze.

A life reduced to turmoil, it's end
a sharp sword's bite.

You don't see the token you are.
Such a bright star,
burst from your father's headache,
you see yourself the better woman-
the wisest there could be, laughing
at Aphrodite's mortal escapades, but
weren't you whispering strategy to Ulysses-
the grey owl forever surveying the battle?
You play her games too, but when you
hold audience with Apollo, you boast of
how you're not like those *other* goddesses.
How you play man's game.
Apollo studies your strong gaze-
your elected dominance and chuckles to himself,
you are a note for him to pluck at endlessly,
his brilliant fingers never growing tired.

Oh, great Mistress Minerva,
You may sit amongst Zeus's counsel,
speak your words true and just, but the feathers
in your helmet are string and your spear only a stick.
And if you were to revolt, what would they say then?
Silly girl, silly girl, leave the war for the men.

Supernova

Have I ever been a fatality-
crumbled a being so completely,
unrecognizable and ashamed?
I wonder if that's what you became.

At the early sparks of our love,
you were an astronomer on the verge
of bottling the newest light in infinity
and now, I can't help but see you
as I had that last time:
broken and finished-
the end so far out of reach,
but never did I hold the goal post away.
Never did I taunt your delayed discovery.
Still the pressure you fabricated persisted
it's beat upon you, your heart could barely hold
onto the burden before you'd self-destruct.
A supernova of your own design,
shattering the Cancer constellation to oblivion.

Damsel

Surrendered to a rocky death,
she is not allowed a choice.
It is he who flies on winged beast
whose destiny proclaims him a savior,
his payment: arms of everlasting gratitude.
But what of Andromeda's will?
Or of Aurora's sleep stopped kiss?
If she were to bolden herself,
to refuse a stranger's touch,
would he release the anger of his rejection-
finding himself clouds away with her
stranded to stone once more?

Would he curse her,
paint her to be an ungrateful hag
or will he say she was placed by the gods- a martyr?
Apollo himself singing of the mortal
who's death a tragedy
as never was there fairer a beauty.

Turns out, she prefers the dragon's bite
to the glimmering shield of a prince.
A dragon remains forever a dragon
and wasn't it Medea who chose
a brimstone mercy to Jason's infidelity?
Let him taste the fear of a woman
eclipsing moonlight,
her flames sacking his statues.
Give him a taste of true humility
and only then, allow him

to don his shield
to hide from his own reflection.

Sisters of the Swan

I sense the loathsome heart
as your names pardon themselves
from tongues unworthy of knowing your fame.
They sneer at how you clasp to your desires-
self-confident: willing yourselves to take
what is yours as your husbands take to their spoils.
Poor wandering piglets, if only Circe had found them
before your dagger's edge, carved so deep- almost beautiful.

The world chose to spit torment-
all it's agony, in your faces for blossoming
into fly traps and when all that rage failed
to vanquish you, they cursed the gods for having
allowed the pair of you to evolve past the cradle.
How dare they allow those faces to peer out
into dawn and dream of kingdoms of majesty.
Yet as much as they play at opposition - they envy you.
In all of history, let it be only you who stole
away from a fate of boredom and possessions.
You gave the fruitless fight for heart,
forced the gods to look from their perch
and say, "now that's different."

Glory is so easily granted to bruiting vessels of war,
those born for their swords and a tyrant's demands, but you-
sisters of the swan, gleam so brightly in Zeus's eyes,
you never let the horizon slip from view,
merely allowing it to linger- eclipsed by ego's head.
Let them drive the gilded horse before the gates,
let them have their fill of plunder and plots,
for when they find themselves home,

you know the Fates are waiting in the wings.
He never accounted for the Spartan's bite.

And what of your revenge do we say?
Nothing beyond the mutterings of a whore.
We merely give you the grievance of man.
But I say, you were merciful in your revenge,
those husbands claiming greats were so fragile,
declaring a war for pride, oh, you could have
looked out from your balcony and laughed,
their army falling before you in shame,
swords sacrificed to sands, shields flung to the sea.
For what were they truly fighting for
if not to reclaim what was never a possession?

Soul of the Sea

I toss myself to the waves,
diving down in search of the ocean's heart,
deep and lost in herself, she is hidden
amidst plastic, *how can she breathe?*

Her currents circle their ancient way
around our sacred plane, yet she's calling
out for someone to grasp her hand-
to pull her out from under,
she can only tread for so long
until she's forced to let go- to sink below,
watching glimmers of light dance among
her children as they circle above-
they don't know to save her.
It's not fair!

She, who caught the sun beneath her waves
to mix our life together with sea foam,
is now drowned by our greed.
> [I cannot let her go, faded like the sun's lazy
> kiss to the horizon, too tired to produce vibrant
> reds today, we're left to settle for a misty yellow
> and clouds left hanging heartbroken.
> I wonder if he cries for her...]

I find her at the bottom, a corpse adorned in coral,
marine life darts in and out of the curve of her back,
her palms caves for morays to lurk.
She's the last reef on earth,
her breath sacrificed for hope that is still fleeting.

Stolen

When my ancestor was taken,
she was not Persephone dripping
pomegranate in the palm of Hell
collecting a kingdom in exchange
six months a haunting.

Persephone came back to see the sun.
She came back to frolic amid daffodils,
to grasp her mother's hand in hers,
to feel the tender kiss of someone
who has gone long without you.

When the bowel of evil washed ashore,
his sight to steal my past's body, he tore
her flesh from the hands she knew–
reduced the memory of her land to shoreline
growing ever farther a   w   a   y-
waves engulfing the sky, a dark hull her horizon.
Wading through foreign fields would never
feel like home, but still you mourn
for Persephone's fruit.

Florida

Lying amongst the storm,
I imagine you a virgin- untouched by outsiders.
Thick woods intertwined with serpentine waterways,
from above you are a maze of green,
parted only by your lover, the sea.
Naiads adorned with lizard earrings bathe in your rivers
as dryads run with panthers under a noisy canopy.
You might not house a fountain of eternal youth,
but the sun kissing your shores refreshes a soul-
reminds us how tiny a speck we remain.
Half a year, you unleash a fury of thunder and might
for you did not permit intruders to harbor in your Eden.
Yet, for all your yelling, we only saw the flowers
growing vibrant from your tears.

Star Catcher

In my dreams, I see him running
anxious to capture the stars falling
around us into the valley.

He pretends the stardust filling his jar
means nothing, "it's for the novelty" he says,
his voice cosmic, words floating out as distant comets
parting the air between us, yet they betray him still.
I can hear the flutters in his chest pulsing
faster as more stars ignite the sky.
For now the stars, which so often scorned his name,
cursed him into the ground, are calling to him-
falling into his arms ready to spill secrets,
giving away the universe to his mind.
He can taste the heaven's kiss,
dance merrily with it in the night.
And I am happy for him,
I wish him all the sky.

The Violinist

You never played for me,
but I remember the way you wore
your violin's case slung to your back
like a burden by a father with deep pocket
dreams for an artist son.
You were more of a doodler,
a sketcher or a philosopher's imagination:
all the colors colliding in an anime
meets steam punk
meets psychedelic trip on paper.

I remember boredom making me bold.
Chemistry wasn't interesting
when I was dealing with teen angst
and broken friendships.
What I wanted was adventure
and the drawings along the corners
of your notes resembled my heartache.

It seemed so easy,
walking up to your desk-
bothering you into liking me.
Turned out we both watched Ghibli,
dreaming of wanderlust as the credits rolled.
You said you wanted to explore Pluto,
so I said, *lets hop in a hot air balloon and go.*
And we went
so many places that sixteenth year until
                              we didn't.

Our destination: a garden
where we had once stolen kisses
on a bench among flowers and metal sculptures.

I imagine crisp autumn air conjured
unease in your winter's heart: it told you
aspire to change, to grow up-
to ditch the daydreamer for the girl
counting down days till graduation, college tours
and a straight path in marine biology.

I remember that walk into Latin,
thinking of how that violin would haunt me-
despite ripping open my soul, you held back
afraid I'd bruise the tender parts of you.
I thought you were Odette hiding a swan curse,
but it was me scorned by the wizard of love.
Leaving me to fly for my life,
unsteady on broken wings.

Labyrinth

With the absence of light,
my soul frequents
dense caverns of mind.
For a time, I am lost unable
to recall life before the maze.

Ariadne, if you're out there,
I could really use you now.

Part Two:
Interludes

Thoughts from the Boat

Screaming at the dark
I forgot how starlight danced among the rain,
a million fairies hailing praise to the night,
the twinkles of Venus beaming down brilliant,
Aurora's breath on far away flowers,
whispering *the dawn arrives in doses,*
shy beyond cloud- afraid to kiss you awake...
remember the sunrise, yellows cool as poolside lemonade,
the first dive off the deep end, waves gently pushing you along.
You will forget his face.
And I wonder how.

Unrequited

Wispy clouds floating overhead
are the unsung hero of morning dew.
They lighten themselves for Aurora's blush
of light only to quietly depart heartbroken,
as she does not notice their affections:
preoccupied by the fairies' dance for her
on the leaves and petals, and song bird's sonnet.
And what of us?
No, as we stir from unrestful sleep,
the hustle we make bustles
too loud to hear tear drops from the sky.

Psyche

We like to imagine it like this:
a lamenting Cupid embracing a fleeting beauty,
her bones roughening against joints,
muscles carving curves of marble,
a final cough of oxygen echoing out in desperation.

She is nearly gone,
having travelled across countryside
into mountain valleys awaiting Hades
for the sake of true love.
> [At birth they sang to her of a princess
> awoken by an angelic lover's kiss.
> And now it is.]

Her eyes opening absorbing his light,
the heavens bestow upon her a starlight destiny.
Love has triumphed again...
Against what evil, they do not say.

We forget her captive nights,
how when the moon is eclipsed by cloud,
a cricket chirps his name,
for she was forbidden to know.
If only she had listened to her sister-
a love which sulks away from light,
could be by no name- no exaggeration-
more than a moment's lust.

And we forget it was he which banished her,
tossed her away for curiosity,
her audacity to seek to know the man

she was bound to by sacrifice.
Why do we give such a loving eye-
why paint his form a beauty
when he's truly the crypt of life
opening the door to darker desires?

When I witness his beastly flesh
carrying away a saddened beauty,
I wish to rip apart his wings-
bind him to the form of a predator
all too frighteningly familiar.
Maybe then we will see.

At the Sea Shore

I was collecting shells-
earnestly stuffing your pail,
thinking you'd find joy in the quantity,
but your little fingers kept insisting
"No, Mama," and tossed them back again
because all the pretty little shells
belonged to the sea
and who were we to keep them?

12:16am

I imagine myself a dwarf star,
quietly outshined by everything else,
glimmering away in the dark.
I blink on silently spewing stardust and radiation
out to no one as not even lost satellites orbit me.
One day, I disappear completely unnoticed
as another light engulfs my absence.
In all that white noise, how could I be heard?
No distant species studies me,
I am without name.
When I blink back into the void,
it doesn't say anything at all-
it has no thoughts on the matter either way.

A Letter from the Sea

You've left me sailing on an unfamiliar sea,
circling islands alone-
you stole my compass, brought night
to the stars, so not even Orion can guide me.
I sail on, wondering how hard it was
to wake to a sea unloving to you.
Each day, you stalked its shores
hungry for a nymph's kiss, but the beach laid barren.
Great Oceanus called his children back to his arms
the moment your eyes smiled at sunrise.
Why couldn't he warn me?
Why couldn't he crash his waves, send his storms-
tell this mortal fool to stay far from blue eyed liars?

The Fates painted you at birth,
screaming little black blooded child- a warning ignored
over the awe of a brother, scarred from the sight.
I can't blame the mother, she was busy,
she didn't hear Lachesis speaking to her sisters,
she didn't hear the pride of their curse,
each nodding before leaving the scene of birth
confident of infidelity- the crimes of Cupid upon your heart.
What could she do if she was listening?

There are mermaids now, sighing amongst
each other before diving amid waves.
They were awaiting some lovelorn sailor
lusting for the wrong flesh, lonely enough
to be taken over by the sirens, unable to cry
in those final moments on the bottom.
A seaweed's kiss goodnight.

Siren teeth on their neck.
I leave their kind on the rocks,
they warn me not to sail on
for Charybdis will swallow me whole
and her mistress Scylla will rip upon me,
but I laugh, knowing if monsters could take me,
I wouldn't have survived you.

They say endurance saves the heart,
I feel it now pounding upon me, unable to break me.
Staring out at horizon, I wonder if I sail far enough
to touch the rim where the sky meets the water,
will I be granted my own wings or cursed to sail as Ulixes?
His ship taking him to the dark before washing
ashore to a home twenty years forgotten.
I wave away his ship of ghosts returning from the pool.
Let me be as Psyche, so I may abandon wayward waters.
I hear the cosmos singing of my constellation,
Hades has an eternity to wait and if your thread
is shorter than mine, send my regards to the boatman.

The Demigods

You dark haired beauties
possess the cunning of an owl-
an ambition to dominate your domain,
the blood of the wolf willing you to love
and annoy one another like asteroids
you clash only to orbit back for hugs.
You are the night meeting day,
popsicles melting against sidewalk,
wishful chalk drawings in September shade.
Two young gods balancing each other's will.

You turn to me, seeing my dark hair- my dark eyes
recognizing that you get so much from me,
except my nose, or my thumb and together
you will wonder where you got those from.
I imagine you'll turn to a book- insisting
you were born from one of my headaches
or hatched like Helen and Clytemnestra.
Or maybe you'll say you weren't born at all.
Your bodies woven by cloud as the cutest,
most perfect beings there ever were
and what a sin it would have been
to not whisk you home as mine.

But that's not how it happened.
That's not how either of you happened.
And I wish I could say that yes, you erupted
from seafoam gleaming as Venus in the late July sun.
I wish that could please you- a simple answer,
but somewhere in you, you'll always wonder where

your father is, having seen the other kids with theirs...
and yes, you only have me,
but I hope when my arms are full
of you and your sister, I'm all you'll ever need.

Empty

You imagine dismantling thoughts
as calculated as machinery- unscrew the cap
and the brain is just one massive gear
twisting to inspire nerves to bounce.
You say one word forms at the mouth
confident others will follow, producing diction.
I wonder, what becomes of the anxious beast
churning over and over at the back of the throat?
"It's simple," you say. "If one gear refuses,
push it until you're satisfied."

Your brain seeks to maximize profit,
process faster, speak with clarity,
enunciate each syllable, their distinct
clicks and clanks never weighted by
more emphasis than any other,
as if you drink from Aletheia's goblet,
every drip of a word floating true and just.

Do you feel empty as your inflection?
Sweet monotone child, you never gain
or lose any more than anticipated.
You could chart your life as an unlabeled graph
and be anything, but your imagery falls
out from your chest as leaves shed from mother trees
in the sunset of the year- beautiful in intention,
                                         a failure to evoke.

Of a Virgo

I thought you were a new star in my sky,
but you have always been an autumnal tide
waiting to be cast away- our visit over
you're sailing back to your constellation,
to drink stardust and dream of someone else.

For a Dog

I try to construct you, sprawled
spring grass, sun bathing bliss,
but the shape of you remains obscure
mingling among smoke and ash.
You will not be swallowed whole
by the deep hunger of Earth-
your spirit ascending
at candle light guided by Hector,
who, recognizing your bravery, rewards you
with gentle pats of gratitude.
The battle of life, at long last, completed.

I Don't Write That Way

I have been cursed by the Fates,
these hands are bound to their works-
my tongue incapable of passing
on its intentions if they are beyond
the arbitrary boundary they have drawn for me.

I will argue with Clotho,
how dare she silence my voice!
No matter how hard a craft is worked-
no matter the years, I may fight my fingers
to bring forth the words, yet there is no life in them.
Only dead air and wasted text.
No matter the books I read, so many thousands
of them staring down at me- I fear some day
I may drown in them, may the great Earth
herself shake them apart from my walls,
bury me beneath them-
swallow me whole as Jonah.
And all the teachers before me
will cry out in that last moment
"you just don't write that way."

Part Three:

Rage

&

the Valley

Off to Young Girls, Every One

(inspired by "Where Have All the Flowers Gone?" by Pete Seeger)

I hear him singing about the flowers,
a field now barren- the weaver's circle
and our walk into the valley.

I imagine those girls charming daisy chains
to adorn another for the sake of innocent
time fading away like the spring.
When you walk in the fields of laughter
you do not see the shadow creeping
just along the horizon, itching to take you
under its great shade for a long sleep.
They do not know to save blossoms for later,
instead they gather until their arms ache
and the wind whistles them home.
They may never learn- a long time passing
before they welcome the shadow,
recognizing it as theirs all along.

Call Me as I Am

Some years ago, a truth echoed
to me across a picnic table,
over potato chips and homework.
"You're the antagonist," he said frank.
Our table shifted in stark silence
folding into aghast as I proudly agreed.
"That's not a good thing," they said,
their side stare slithering away in caution.
How could I lie, when that skinny child
drowning in flannel, who smelled of bagged herb
and moldy bread could name me so completely?

I was never a hero, allow Achilles
to win his victories blooded on foreign field-
his death is not for me.
I'm hardly Ulysses,
though woven by cunning cloth,
when called from thought for your unworthy advance,
I settle myself still, a statue unmovable.
Never a pledge be made on my heart
for another's fragility.

Somehow, I remain without villainy-
though maybe in your story I'm different.
I can't tell you how to write me.
May you call me demon,
proclaim there's something deeply wronged in me,
my curiosities unsettle you-
my sight alone a burden on your lofty soul.
When you ask why I walk against your path,

do not feign surprise.
I'll gladly settle for Antigone's cave.
She was hers,
as I am still wholly mine.

Sword in the Forge

You are a sword still with the smith.
The years beaten down on you
only made you stronger- refined.
You have always been something fierce,
time only opened the geode of your heart,
pulled forth an emerald core
and let the Fates smile upon you.
You are smooth metal worth more than starlight-
you couldn't farm rage this pure.
You wear your sheath, may it be a curtesy
or warning for those to rue their prophecy.

When I Was the Tree and You Were the Sky

We rested under a warm canopy
shaded from tones of autumn,
our hair tangled with leaves.
You stared unchanged while I watched
wondering what made you cold-
why you laid silent without response
to my thoughts, as if yours were better
abstracted puffs of cloud sorting through possibilities.
I had thought we were the trees and the sky:
your pale luminescent eyes shifted to new theory
as my branches begging hazel stretched to reach you,
your chilling breath stirring leaves floating skyward...
yet, they slipped
through wispy fingertips and I couldn't feel an attempt
to catch me, though I hope it was there once,
flittering around in your mind among so much else,
Catch me. Please, catch me.
I know now, there was no desire to pull me into you,
to melt our thoughts among the other-
blended then reborn: a chimera.
Your refusal folded our existence into memory,
separated on a singular horizon, you above
and I destined to keep looking upward.

Mixed

I don't know what I am,
pulled in so many directions...
which shore should I rest on?
The Old World, land of kings,
a hall of eternal sunshine,
conspiracy & greed- an executioner's end.
A tropic island battered by the storm-
we are strong, rebuilding, unwavering.
A West African shore: too far
to recall, close enough to cry.
My hands unmoving on the paddle.
I'm lost, unable to row.

I struggle to find Limbo's edge,
to reach out to those ancestors left behind
in the past, but they won't catch me
and I can't handle their rejection-
their proclamation that while our blood
runs the same red, my face isn't their own.
I am a mangled host of souls messily stitched together.
I hope it is all an imagining.
A resting death harbors no ill nature,
instead it is the living who see me
                                      and stop.
But you don't speak Spanish,
But your dad is white,
I thought you were French,
You should stop lying,
Stop talking, white girl!
You don't look mixed.

I wonder, if I look like every other
Irish girl born in some wheat field,
drinking overpriced lattes,
sharing inspirational garbage on Facebook,
does that offend you?
That I blend in?
That when your mother told me
if I hate America so much,
I should go back to where I came from
and I said "I'm sorry, where should that be?
These lands have always been mine."
You flushed, embarrassed.
You didn't know- you thought
I was your own, when I have always been
the stranger in your flesh.

Return to the Forest

On a July day, four of us took
to hike through a forest forgotten to me.
My sixteenth year kept memory of each leaf,
a hymn of tender sunshine under canopy.
I thought these woods ancient.
Wandering through that day
I recognized the oddity of man
placing his structures where they ought not be.
Did no one notice, but me, the strangeness of air?
The yoga pants, Pokémon trainers,
and underpaid dog walkers?
I thought we would echo Thoreau's trek to a pond,
study its waters, breathe life as we had never been
connected like mushrooms to a bigger system before,
but I found you busy catching the imaginary,
shouting profanity,
leaving me and my explorer's heart
to witness tadpoles scoot along alone.

Response to the Sound of Trees

When Frost complained of the noise of his trees,
I wonder, had he never experienced a summer
plagued by the nonsense bound to vacationing cicadas?
At least his trees spoke of adventure,
these annoying drones of heat and misadventure
start up their groaning so early an hour,
I fear the sun himself is forced from his bed
due to their skittering voice, going on and on again.
They are that that talks of nothing, and never goes away.
They talk with no sense of knowing as they grow wiser and
older-once they come they mean to stay, basking beneath
the summer sun until Helios no longer holds back his anguish-
extinguishing them in a final swoop of a season,
bringing upon us late September silence.
A joy, for the constant headache of summer has its end.

Romeo & Juliet

We call them star-crossed
idiots for Cupid's unchanging arrow-
how his pin prinks of lust
throbbed upon their heart.
They could not see a sunrise amidst
their desire and fated they were
to stew in turmoil.
We are a blind intruder
to their tale, judging with bitter heart.
When did we become this hardened-
beaten into seclusion from the pursuit
to know another's shape among starlight?

A cynical mouth cannot paint
the beauty of a rose.
And they tried.
The adornment of death,
flushed their cheeks, a quiet peace
overtaking their once desolate reality.
We bemoan the waste of life,
but as they hold another in their crypt
it is only us who remain alone.

Ally

I wash ashore broken
as shade speckled by stubborn sun,
watching the sea beside me stretching endless.
Waves tossing surf, remnants of my boat
bobbing with the water's dance.
I feel I could give up,
my soul escaping with every sigh.
Where can I go from here?
But then I see it, golden on the hill.
You peer out anxious, eyeing the wreckage.
Athena at my ear sings *catch the pieces-*
find their place before falling in Loki's light.
Arise again.
And I pick up my fight.

Each step to your castle sure as thunder,
I remember the Fates proclaimed me the ally.
The sword they crafted came gripped
firmly in my hands as a storm surged- a coward,
jealous I won the fight of birth.
As I grew, my sword followed me,
a mighty cleaver envied by Artemis.
She ran with me through my grandmother's roses
and shared wild blackberries in July's bliss.
At night, my soul danced among ancestors
under starlight, their tender embrace
decorating me with Ursa Major and Minor,
duality tuning the beast in me- subdued and blazing.
You followed treason home, now witness
her poison spread as I cast the lips of sky
open to engulf the pity of you forever.

I am here, rapping upon your door.

They say you are he which grabs at the heel,
but I am not Achilles,
I am not so easily discarded from the story.
Step off the throne- shed the goat from your back
and reveal your true skin, flushed pink- unloved by the sun.
I wonder, do you wallow in your burns
or are you ignorant to think they adorn you clever?

No Return Receipt

You once told me,
while in the pit of your despair,
that you wasted your years on me.

I've thought it over,
turning those words round in my head,
twisting them in different lights,
so that I may see as you do...
Six years gone and you speak your words
as if you can return love lost
like an impulse buy at Target.
That's not how it works.

Kisses can not be taken back
nor drowsy conversations in the dark.
You cannot cloth yourself once you've borne
your silenced soul to the stars, as I cannot pretend
those words weren't spoken from your lips,
distain flooding through the phone-
did you think I wouldn't hear?

Six years and they're to be tossed back to you?
You'd have better luck with the sea.
Let it toil itself endlessly for you,
with each break of a wave,
there's sea foam in your face.
Let it bare itself out for you and see
how kindly Poseidon takes your return receipt.

Our chapter clasped shut
as clams guarding their pearls-
gone before I knew it, the waves
pushing us forward secretly marked
by years spent among the other,
things we may never get over,
things we would rather hide-
let time forget...
for that is the gamble I make for love,
forever tossing my soul out to sea
while you're lost in your own odyssey
cursing the sky, for even the sun has turned
to December at the sight of you,
I will vow for love- it will come back to me.

In the Valley of the Dead

Shakespeare once told me
"these violent delights have violent ends."
I see it now, in the children ripped
from mothers, their little fingers clawing for air.
Cries echoing away to nowhere,
playing on and on again- we forget their face,
their desperation and defeat, yet I linger,
wondering what has been their crime.
We have shipped them away, only dust remains
in a place that once cradled a family.
Do they not deserve the pursuit of happiness?

The children of the past crawl
out from the mud, their tired eyes
sullen as dusk, pulling forth an anger.
We have stolen from them a life
we so desperately claimed our right- drawn
them across the south- we knew the littlest
could not survive the journey, but still we persisted,
pulling apart a spirit mile by mile until they dropped.
Bones so small, they could be sea shells.

We shamed them to camps unseen.
We still justify- *It was us against an enemy
hiding within,* but they were our own-
not some child across the sea.
Their first sight was our sky, yet still
we cast their dreams to night.
And what has been their crime?

I ask again, for the children who will
not come home to meet their mother's arms.
The badges will say they were carrying a knife,
but even the shopkeeper says it was a Snickers.
Face down in a parking lot, 12 years old.
What has been their crime?

Looking upon that great house built
by the hands of a nameless people,
I know when we walk through
the shadow of the valley of death,
we will fear no evil, for we have become evil.
Were you not once a stranger in Egypt?

America

We beckon you from ships
weather battered from the storm-
decay and carnage seas away.

Our goddess, our beacon, begging you
to harbor among her shores, but your gaze
cannot steer away from the blood-soaked soil,
brown children crying for a father painted monster.
"He was only walking," they say.
Grandmothers carrying them away,
silent for the tears staining their voice.
They have to bury another son, another father,
another bright-eyed child eager to shine,
but we were fearful their light.

You decline to depart the vessel.
You were told this was the land of the free,
but staring into Liberty's eyes, so clearly now,
you can see they're empty, simply painted
glass to shine out artificial light- her soul
departed long before, her body a casket
for all those dreams left rotting at her gates,
rats climb her legs.
This is America?
and we laugh, "Didn't you know?"
The demons in suit jackets count you
like dollars in their wallet- they will never
give back, eager to eat you whole,
strip you bare upon the soil and when they're done,
toss you away like the rest- an unmarked grave.

To the Conquistador

I am the Fury of revenge,
ignited by the bodies of my dead.
Your ships sailed to slaughter,
a coughing sickness,
swords and rage fueled greed.
We could adorn you Midas and still,
our gold could not satisfy a pride
that glistens off a silver chest plate,
a broken compass and a lack of mind.
My ancestor stood strong among decay.
She said, *we will rise again*.
She said, *you may steal our land,*
but we will steal your body.
You laughed
then worked her to death.

And here I am,
Your reckoning in white.
Don't you recognize me?
My high cheeks and dark locks.
Don't you recognize me?
The dark eyes and five hundred years
of fury bound in a small frame.
Don't you recognize me?
I'm white as the tunnel of death.

End of an Era

Do not call me Mary,
I've been painted her before:
stoic, silent, grieving for a sign of dawn.
We are not the same, though I lack
a desire to claw her off a golden throne,
reduce her statues to unremarkable marble,
sack the churches she calls home, like the lion she isn't:
please care to distinguish this unfiltered tongue from hers.

My hands will not call upon angels to decide fate for me.
I will grab the sword, raise it proudly on the hill-
its blade reflecting glory as I charge
unflinching toward my own demons.
Leave yours at home,
locked away for your own prayers to take away.

I am stubborn, self-righteous and unafraid
of the divinity which flows through me.
I have forged it with my own hands,
dug my own castle from the mud- dirty and black,
and you may claim my hubris, but I can't care to listen.
I'm tired of the words falling from lazy mouths granted
dignity by what lay between their legs- you are not a king.
And I have heard you laugh at Lucy's claim,
that she will buy herself a queendom,
naming it yet another silly thing we do.
But who's to say she cannot plot her place among the crowns?
Or is that place reserved for brutes, liars, colonizers,
and pea-brained money bred leaches
which suckle on suffering, fire and greed?
I say no.

Take care to listen for my battle cry,
its distant call to you from the mountains,
your feeble frame unprepared for the avalanche.
You will see the Valkyrie riding, and it's then,
ashamed of your cowardice, you see us rise
while your pack cru m
             b
           l
                    e
                              s.

Glossary of Gods, Heroes & Beasts

Greek & Roman

Achilles- declared the greatest fighter of all Greek heroes past and future, Achilles was a demigod known for his involvement and drama in Homer's Iliad. Having refused to fight for the Greeks as having disagreed with Agamemnon's politics, he only returned to the battlefield after his lover, Patroclus, stole his armor and was subsequently murdered by Hector on the field. He sought revenge for his lover's death by destroying Hector in hand to hand combat. He then pulled Hector's body behind his chariot in disrespect. Achilles was ultimately defeated by Paris, who shot an arrow through his only weakness, his heel. In the Odyssey, Odysseus visits Achilles at the pool of the dead, where he expresses deep regret for living fast and dying young.

Agamemnon & Menelaus- sons of Atreus (king of Mycenae) and husbands to Clytemnestra and Helen. Agamemnon led the Trojan War to restore his brother's honor and plunder Troy of its riches. Their story is told in Homer's Iliad and Odyssey.

Alethea/ Aletheia- the goddess of truth.

Andromeda- daughter of the mortal queen, Cassiopeia, who boasted her daughter was more beautiful than the Nereids (the daughters of Poseidon.) Having offended the sea god, he demanded Andromeda be sacrificed to the sea monster, Cetus. She was later saved by Perseus on his way back from slaying Medusa. This story is where we get the princess and the dragon motif in many medieval fairytales.

Antigone- daughter of Oedipus and his mother, Jocasta. In Sophocles' play of the same name, she is sentenced to be buried alive in a cave for giving proper burial rites to her brother. Her uncle, the new ruler after the demise of Oedipus, decreed that her brother was to be shamed and bared from receiving the rites, thus making Antigone's action treason. She stood by her decision when questioned and accepted her fate.

Aphrodite/ Venus- goddess of beauty and mother of Cupid. She was born from sea foam following Cronus' defeat of his father, Uranus. She had many escapades with mortal and gods. She is most notable for helping start the Trojan war in Homer's Iliad. She gifted Helen to Paris as a reward for him saying she was the most beautiful goddess, thus ending a feud started by Eris (goddess of discord.) She was also the only Olympian to side with the Trojans in the war.

Apollo- twin of Artemis, he was the god of the arts (music, poetry, visual arts) as well as prophecy, knowledge, archery and the sun (among many other things.) He was the god invoked by the Oracle of Delphi (otherwise known as Pythia.) He pops up time and time again in mythology, most notably in Homer's Iliad where he sends a plague to the Greek camps in response to Agamemnon taking one of his priest's daughters as a spoil of war.

Ariadne- daughter of the mortal king, Minos and his goddess wife, Pasiphae. Ariadne was the sister of the Minotaur and lover of Theseus. In myth, she gave Theseus his sword and a spool of thread, so he could find his way back out of the labyrinth. In some accounts, she was the wife of Dionysus.

Artemis- twin of Apollo, she was the virgin goddess of the hunt, wilderness and animals. She was also considered the protector of women.

Athena/ Minerva- goddess of wisdom, war strategy and justice (among other things.) She appears in many myths, though notably she helped Odysseus in Homer's Iliad and Odyssey, as she favored the Greeks in the Trojan War.

Atlas- a Titan condemned to hold up the sky for eternity as punishment for fighting with the Titans in the war between the Titans and Olympians.

Aurora- goddess of the dawn. She was the sibling of the sun (Sol) and the moon (Luna.) In mythology, she loved a mortal prince whom she asked Jupiter (Zeus) to grant immortality to. Unfortunately, she forgot to ask the he be granted eternal youth as well. When he grew old, she transformed him into a cicada.

Cerberus- the three headed dog charged with guarding the Underworld to stop the dead from leaving.

Charybdis- a giant whirlpool located in the Strait of Messina. She is often referenced in Homer's Odyssey.

Circe- daughter of the sun god, Helios. She was the goddess of sorcery and transmutation. Her most notable appearance in mythology is in Homer's Odyssey, where she turns Odysseus' men into pigs, only to later help him on his quest back to Ithaca.

Cupid- son of Venus and Mars, he was the god of love and affection. He is most notable in the myth of Cupid and Psyche.

Dryad- the general term for a tree nymph.

The Fates- three goddesses of life, destiny and death. Clotho, the weaver of the thread of life. She controlled central points to a person's being, like when they were born etc. Lachesis, the measurer of the thread. She controlled destiny. Atropos, the cutter of the thread. She controlled how someone dies and when the time came (as decided by Lachesis) she cut the thread.

The Furies- three goddesses of vengeance. Alecto punished moral crimes. Megaera punished those guilty of infidelity, broken promises and thievery. Tisiphone punished murderers.

Hades- god of the Underworld. After the war between the Olympians and Titans, he was chosen to oversee the realm of the dead. In mythology, he stole Persephone from a flower field and she is forced to spend half the year with him.

Hector- a Trojan prince noted as the greatest fighter for Troy. He was killed in a duel with Achilles after mistakenly murdering Patroclus.

Helen and Clytemnestra- twin daughters of the mortal queen, Leda. They (along with their brothers Castor and Pollux) were the product of the Leda's Swan myth, though only Helen is a daughter of Zeus. Helen was declared the most beautiful woman in the world by the goddess, Aphrodite. She later stole away with Paris to Troy for unclear reasons. Some accounts say she was kidnaped by Paris, others say she chose to leave her husband, Menelaus. Clytemnestra was betrayed by her husband, Agamemnon when he sacrificed their daughter to Artemis in exchange for safe voyage to Troy. She began a love affair while her husband was at war and upon his return, she avenged her daughter's death by murdering him.

Helios- Titan of the sun. His chariot pulls the sun into the sky each day.

Heracles- in myth, he was the son of Zeus and a mortal woman. He was renowned for his super human strength. At birth, Hera tried to kill him by sending snakes after him, but baby Heracles strangled them. Later in his life, Hera sent him into a blind rage, where he murdered his wife and children. From this we have the Labors of Heracles, a series of impossible tasks his half-brother sent him on. These trials included slaying the Nemean Lion, slaying the Hydra, stealing the Apples of Hesperides, and capturing Cerberus and bringing him out of the Underworld.

Medusa- a former priestess of Athena. She was brutally raped by Poseidon in Athena's temple. For the disgrace, Athena transformed her into a Gorgon. If anyone laid an eye on her, they turned to stone. She was eventually killed by Perseus, as he was tasked to retrieve her head in exchange for his mother.

The Muses- the nine daughters of Zeus and Mnemosyne (the goddess of memory,) they personified arts and culture. Calliope, muse of epic poetry. Cleo, muse of history. Euterpe, muse of lyric poetry. Thalia, muse of comedy. Melpomene, muse of tragedy. Terpsichore, muse of dance. Erato, muse of love poems. Polyhymnia, muse of sacred poetry. Urania, muse of astronomy.

Naiads- water nymphs that primarily presided over fountains and freshwater.

Narcissus- a hunter of profound beauty, he was tricked by Nemesis to view himself in a pool of water. He fell in love with his image and never looked away.

Nereids- water nymphs that specifically inhabited the Mediterranean Sea.

Nymphs- a term for lesser goddesses.

Oceanids- salt water nymphs, they presided over the ocean.

Oceanus- Titan of the sea. His children are the Naiads.

Orion- a great hunter who was slain by a scorpion sent by the goddess, Gaia. She felt he would go on to kill every beast on the planet if no one stopped him. His body was placed among the stars by Zeus on the request of his friend, Artemis.

Orpheus- son of the muse, Calliope. He was an excellent musician. In myth, he travelled to the Underworld to convince Hades and Persephone to let him bring his wife back to the world of the living. Using the lyre he was gifted by Apollo, his music persuaded them, but with a catch. He had to walk in front of her on the journey back. Should he look back, she would vanish forever. In anxiety and excitement, he forgot just as he reached the top, having looked back only for his wife to disappear for good.

Persephone- Queen of the Underworld and goddess of spring. She was kidnapped by her uncle, Hades and is subsequently forced to spend half the year in the Underworld with him.

Poseidon- god of the sea, earthquakes and horses. He appears numerous times in mythology, mostly when he rapes or is upset with a mortal.

Psyche- a mortal princess turned goddess of the soul. In mythology, she was sacrificed to marry a mysterious monster who came to her each night under the cover of darkness. Out of curiosity, one night she lit a candle only to find it was a god (Cupid) sleeping beside her. She was then cursed to walk the earth until her death, where Cupid came to her again and for her devotion to him, he made her a goddess. Her symbol is the butterfly. You can read her story in Till We Have Faces by C.S. Lewis.

Scylla- a multi-headed sea monster positioned on a cliff beside Charybdis. She devours sailors seeking to get by the whirlpool. She is specifically referenced in Homer's Odyssey.

Ulysses/ Ulixes/ Odysseus- one of the many Greek heroes to fight for Agamemnon in the Trojan war. He was notable for his plan and execution of the Trojan Horse. Homer's Odyssey follows his perilous journey back home to his kingdom of Ithaca after the war.

Zeus- god of the sky and thunder. He led the revolution to free his siblings from the belly of his father, Cronus. With the help of some Titans, the Olympians won the war, solidifying Zeus as the king of all gods. In mythology, Zeus is often seen as unfaithful to his wife/sister, Hera. Many gods and heroes in Grecian myth are children of Zeus, much to Hera's displeasure. This is the crux of many conflicts in Grecian mythology.

Norse

Loki- god of mischief. In myth, he plays an integral role in starting Ragnarok.

The Valkyrie- a band of women led by Freyja. The appeared during a battle to decide the fate of those fighting. Of the slain, they chose who went to Valhalla.

Acknowledgements:

I want to extend a thank you to the following, your existence in some way helped make this the book it is today.

Mom, thank you for telling me stories about yourself growing up. When I think of a strong woman, I think of that time you took down a man taller than you. He didn't realize the fury of a small woman. I hope to channel at least half your fire.

Madeline, your thoughtful critiques of my poetry helped point me in the right direction when I desperately needed it.

Netflix, for your endless supply of children's programming. This book was written through many reruns of PJ Masks, Chuggington and Pocoyo.

Ambur & Louise, your combined reaction to the daily news cycle introduced me to Exodus 23:9 and thus helped me vocalize my feelings towards our country's brutality towards immigrants and those claiming asylum.

Dad, thank you for your insistence in watching the news, even though we already know what'll be on…more coverage of the Trumpster Fire, yet another mass shooting and how we're all angry, but not doing anything about it. I'm tired of the garbage we're being given. My poetry is my revolt until someone busts out a guillotine.

The rest of my family (though I will specifically name Sean and Lena,) thank you for all the support you gave my first collection.

And you the reader, this book would be nothing without a reader. I thank you for spending your hard-earned dollars on my words. God knows you need it in this economy.

About the Author

Dakota Boyer is a poet from Florida who will adamantly agree, that yes, Florida is a shithole, but no, we do not ride Alligators down the street. And that you don't really see that many of them up in northern Florida, but its still probably not a good idea to go swimming in the rivers. Actually, you might want to double check the pool too. Did you know, Alligators can climb fences? Yes, you read that right. They climb fences. When she's not writing, Dakota is eager to supply useless facts to an unsuspecting victim, read the next book on her to be read list or chase her toddlers around the house. Dakota graduated from Douglas Anderson School of the Arts where she studied creative writing. Her interests include Japanese Street Fashion, nature, astronomy, mythology, poetry, existentialism (minus the dread,) and letter board pictures on Instagram. Of Violent Delights is her second poetry collection, following close behind Edge of Stardust which was published in May 2018.

You can find her on Instagram @thunderousdandelion.

Made in the USA
Columbia, SC
11 January 2025